STUFF
EVERY
ADULT
SHOULD
KNOW

Library of Congress Control Number: 2024945131

ISBN: 978-1-68369-479-3

Printed in China

Typeset in Adobe Garamond Pro and Figtree

Designed by Paige Graff
Illustrations on pages 59, 61, 75, 77–78, and 82 by Kate Francis
Illustrations on pages 64–65, 68–70, and 85 by Vic Kulihin
Production management by Mandy Sampson

Quirk Books
215 Church Street
Philadelphia, PA 19106
quirkbooks.com

10 9 8 7 6 5 4 3 2 1

Stuff Every Lawyer Should Know: The publisher and authors hereby disclaim any liability from an injury that may result from the use, proper or improper, of the information contained in this book. We do not guarantee that this information is safe, complete, or wholly accurate, nor should it be considered a substitute for a reader's good judgment and common sense.

STUFF
EVERY
ADULT
SHOULD
KNOW

QUIRK BOOKS
PHILADELPHIA

WORK AND MONEY STUFF

INTERPERSONAL STUFF

INTRODUCTION

Almost nobody actually feels like an adult. And yet, at some point, almost all of us start being expected to act like one. People stop rescuing you from your own mistakes. They stop cleaning up after you. They stop telling you what the heck you're supposed to be *doing.* You start having to take responsibility for things like work and taxes and cleaning and your health and the health of houseplants and animals and even actual babies (but *you're* the baby!). And sometimes it seems like everyone else is just breezing through and you're the only fraud.

But again, almost nobody feels like an adult—we promise! Because adulthood isn't a feeling. It's a set of skills. And if you don't have those skills, you can get them. In fact, getting the adulthood skills you don't have yet is one of the most important adulthood skills.

That means you're on the right track, and you're in the right place.

This book probably can't solve every single one of your grown-up problems. But it can give you enough background knowledge that when life throws adult stuff at you—a tire you have to change, a lease you have to sign, a button you have to replace, a baby you have to hold—you won't feel like you're starting from zero. And there's fun stuff in here, too, about making friends and throwing dinner parties and finding a cause you believe in! Adulthood isn't all chores and insurance forms.

People probably still won't clean up after you, or save you from your mistakes, at least after the first ten or fifteen—but we lied when we said nobody would tell you what the heck you're supposed to *do*. We'll tell you! It's all here.

SELF-CARE
STUFF

How to De-Stress

Stress is one of the biggest contributors to disease. Although this feeling can be a powerful motivator, you should have a way to shake off too much tension before it snowballs into something more serious.

- How you respond to and handle stress is an indication of what you need to do to remedy it. If not much fazes you, you might just need to sit down with a book and a cup of tea, watch TV, or do anything else that will let your brain turn to mush for a while.

- On the other hand, if you tend to internalize stress, become increasingly tense, lose sleep, and snap at people for no reason, you'll need to be a little more proactive. The first step is to learn to identify when you are entering that mode, so your stress-induced misery doesn't blindside you and prevent you from doing something about it.

- Exercise is a major ally in battling stress. You might not be able to punch that incompetent moron from Marketing in the face, but you can direct all that energy to a punching bag or an exhausting run. Making your body work hard will help relieve some of the pressure that's plaguing you.

- Many people say they are happier and less stressed when they eat healthful foods. Fruits, veggies, and whole grains naturally give you more energy, whereas junk food can actually raise your stress levels.

- The fascinating thing about stress is that we do it to ourselves. Tough as it is, you can choose whether or not to let something get to you. Since that won't happen overnight, find activities that are soothing and distracting. Long walks, deep breathing, talking to a friend, gardening, crossword puzzles, yoga, painting, taking a bath, sitting on a park bench and soaking up the sun, volunteering, going for a drive and blasting music—anything that lets you focus on something else for a bit.

- Get enough sleep, find a few hours a week for exercise, and devote twenty minutes a day to something relaxing. Taking care of yourself is the ultimate gift you can give yourself, and you'll be a happier, healthier person for it.

How to Deal with Depression

Though it often seems like everyone else is doing fine, depression is common. According to a 2021 survey by the National Institute of Mental Health, more than 8 percent of adults—and more than 18 percent of people ages 18 to 25—report having had a major depressive episode in the previous year. That's literally millions of people. *You are not alone.* Many of us experience this feeling of loss or sadness. Here's how to make your mental health a priority.

DEAL WITH YOUR DAMN FEELINGS

1. **Be aware of your damn feelings.** Common symptoms of depression include (but are not limited to) a sense of hopelessness or helplessness; changes in sleep patterns, appetite, and weight; loss of energy; decreased interest in daily activities; problems with concentration; feelings of self-hatred; and suicidal thoughts. You might not experience all these symptoms, but recognize that this state of mind isn't something you can just shake off.

2. **Share your damn feelings.** You might want nothing more than to stay under the covers for

a cartoon-watching marathon, but force yourself to hang out with friends (or, you know, invite them over to watch cartoons). Tell family members what you're going through and ask them for advice. Don't feel embarrassed about needing help. Depression is isolating, but having a caring support system goes a long way toward making you realize you are not alone.

3. **Talk to a therapist about your damn feelings.** Therapy can be extremely helpful, and seeking help is *not* an admission of defeat, weakness, or insanity. Research local services (*Psychology Today* offers an online search engine of providers, as do many insurance companies) to find someone who works with young adults or your specific situation. You might not find a good fit right away, so try a few therapists until you both "click."

AND DON'T FORGET TO . . .

- **Take care of yourself.** Doing nice things for yourself is a matter of self-preservation, not self-indulgence. Make happiness your top priority. Listen to your favorite music. Bake brownies.

Play Tetris, knit a sweater. Whatever raises your spirits.

- **Avoid self-medicating.** Don't use alcohol or drugs to deal with how you're feeling. You might think these will bring immediate stress relief, but in the long run substance abuse is likely to deepen and may in fact *cause* depression.

- **Be patient.** Remember that life doesn't fall into place right away. Jobs take a while to materialize. Friends move away. Parents can be overbearing. Maybe you feel like you've taken a massive step backward, but don't despair. Life doesn't always move consistently forward or at a constant pace. You're doing fine.

How to Get a Good Night's Sleep

Restful sleep is essential for recharging your body and setting you up for a successful day. If you have trouble getting enough shut-eye, consider these suggestions.

- **Create a daily sleep schedule.** Get in the habit of going to sleep and waking at the same time. This will create a sleep/wake cycle for your body, and with time, you may train yourself to wake without an alarm clock. Waking naturally may also make you feel more rested and ready for the day.

- **Consider your environment.** Find a room temperature that works for your body. Eliminate distractions like lights and noises. Tidy up your bedroom if the mess adds stress (and remember to make your bed). Employ a sound machine if background noise helps you doze off.

- **Manage your daily lighting.** Sunlight or bright light can increase your energy during the day while also improving your sleep quality at night. On the other hand, exposure to intense lighting at night tricks your brain into thinking it's daytime and reduces your melatonin level, which helps your body relax. So increase bright light exposure during the day, and decrease blue light exposure in the evening by putting your phone and other electronic devices away well before bedtime.

- **Be mindful of caffeine, sugar, and alcohol.** Elevated levels of caffeine stimulate your nervous system and prevent your body from relaxing. Because caffeine can stay in your blood for up to eight hours, minimizing or eliminating consumption after noon can contribute to better sleep. Sugary foods should also be avoided in the evening for similar reasons. Additionally, alcohol is known to disrupt sleep by altering melatonin production.

- **Develop a bedtime relaxation routine.** Do something that clears your mind and helps your body relax. Take a hot bath or a shower. Listen to calming music. Meditate. Read a book. Try different things to find what works best for you.

- **Know how to fall back asleep.** It's normal to wake up in the middle of the night. If you have trouble falling back asleep, try to avoid stressing about it. Instead, take slow deep breaths, or practice progressive muscle relaxation techniques, in which you tense and relax each muscle in your body one at a time. These will help you relax your body without overstimulating your brain.

- **Consult a doctor.** If you have trouble sleeping, you should speak to a doctor to rule out a sleep disorder. Additionally, your doctor may recommend over-the-counter supplements such as melatonin or prescribe something stronger to help you sleep.

How to Care for Your Skin

Fun fact: Your skin is your largest organ. And it's the one that's most exposed to the effects of the outside world. Follow this simple routine to protect your skin while keeping your face looking clean and healthy.

1. Wash your face once or twice daily. Do this to remove all the dirt on your face. A normal bar of soap will dry your skin out, causing it to create more oils. So, opt for a gentle, hydrating soap specifically designed for use on your face. Wash your face in the morning when you wake up, as your pillow is a hotbed for bacteria. Cleanse again prior to going to bed if you have oily skin.

2. Exfoliate once per week. After you wash your face, use a gentle face scrub to clear away any dead skin, open your pores, and bring the healthier skin cells to the surface.

3. Moisturize your skin. Once you've cleaned your face and removed all the dirt, bacteria, and dead skin cells, you'll want to rehydrate and protect your face. A moisturizer will deliver vitamins and nutrients to the skin while also hydrating it and preventing it from creating excess oil. Apply

the moisturizer to a dry face once or twice daily after washing and/or exfoliating.

4. Protect yourself from the sun. Apply sunscreen with SPF 30 when you will be outside for extended periods. It will block harmful UV rays that lead to sunspots, wrinkles, sunburns, moles, and cancer. Often, the SPF is built into a moisturizer that can perform double duty.

> **Note:** If you have dry or oily skin, adult acne, or other skin conditions, you should speak to a dermatologist, who can provide individualized skincare treatment.

How to Stay in Shape

You know exercise is good for you, but whether you're starting a stressful new job or spending a lot of time with Netflix, maintaining a fitness regimen can be tough. Here's how to defeat laziness and keep yourself going strong.

- Know yourself: If you prefer to work out alone, try swimming laps, cycling, or a one-on-one boxing lesson. If you'd rather be part of a group, a water-aerobics class or swim team, runners' group, or basketball league might be better. If you have bad knees, asthma, or depth perception problems, or if you need a wheelchair-friendly activity, research the types of exercise that will work for you to narrow down your options and keep you safe.

- The fancy gym with the army of personal trainers might be tempting, but community rec centers and YMCA chapters will almost always be cheaper. Universities may offer classes to local nonstudents, and yoga studios often have pay-what-you-can community classes for charity. If budgets can't budge, pick up an inexpensive gym mat and take to YouTube for exercise videos.

- Pressed for time? Try a circuit workout: 30 seconds each of jumping jacks, wall sits, push-ups, chair step-ups, squats, triceps chair dips, ab planks, running in place, and lunges, with 10-second breaks in between. Phew!

- Fit exercise into your schedule wherever it makes sense, even if it's a quick 30-minute session during a lunch break or a late-night yoga class to relax before bed. If the workout is convenient, you're more likely to do it.

- Workouts that fulfill two objectives may be easier to stick with. Joining an amateur softball league will win you new friends. Dance classes can double as quality couple time. Treadmill workouts are opportunities to catch up on Netflix or podcasts.

- Don't feel intimidated. Exercise is literally for every body, whether you're a former teenage athlete or you've never run a mile in your life. Lots of people start new sports as adults, so head to that roller derby info session. If you're nervous, talk to the instructor beforehand—they'll love an eager newcomer.

- Don't get down on yourself. If you lapse a little, the least helpful thing is to beat yourself up. Just move on and start fresh.

How to Take Care of Yourself When You're Sick

Since the last thing you want to do when you're bed-ridden is make complicated self-care decisions, here are some quick tips for combatting common ailments.

COLDS

- Blow your nose instead of sniffing the phlegm back into your body.

- Gargle with warm salt water.

- Clear your sinuses by taking a hot shower; or put your face over a bowl of very hot water, and cover both your head and the bowl with a towel.

- Drink lots of fluids.

- Wash your hands as often as possible.

- Eat foods that are easy on a sore throat, like soups and applesauce.

- Opt for nondrowsy daytime cold medicine if you need to stay alert, and sleep-friendly formulas when you want to catch some Z's.

- Clear your nasal passages using a neti pot and sinus rinse (available at most pharmacies; be sure to use distilled water or water that's been boiled and cooled to avoid parasites).

FLUS

- As with a cold, hydrate, gargle, and unclog your sinuses.

- Prevention goes a long way: get a seasonal flu shot and COVID vaccine, wash your hands frequently, and stay away from that one coworker who showed up looking like a zombie.

- *Stay home.* Wait a full 24 hours after a fever abates before resuming your normal schedule.

- Try to eat a little something, even if you lack an appetite. A bit of soup or plain rice can help keep up your strength.

FEVERS

- Get a thermometer (before you get sick, *ahem!*) and monitor your temperature to make sure it's returning to normal (98.6°F; 37°C).

- Rest and drink plenty of water. Popsicles will work.

- Both ibuprofen and acetaminophen can lower a fever, and most drug stores stock fever-specific options. Be sure to read all labels carefully.

- If you've got the chills, resist the urge to bundle up too much—you'll only increase your body temperature. Taking a lukewarm bath can help.

- Call a doctor if the fever doesn't respond to medication, is consistently above 103°F (39.4°C), or lasts for more than three days.

MENSTRUAL PAIN

- Stretching and yoga can help cramps. Also comforting are hot compresses or an electric heating pad applied to your lower abdomen. Make your own compress by filling a sock with uncooked rice and knotting the opening; microwave it for 1–2 minutes.

- Avoid alcohol and caffeine, which can dehydrate you and worsen symptoms.

- Take it easy. If you suffer from severe PMS, set a calendar alert to remind yourself to ease up and slow down.

- NSAIDs like ibuprofen or naproxen (not acetaminophen) will lessen uterine muscle contractions as well as leg, back, and head pain. You can use these medicines preventatively, too, but don't exceed the daily maximum dosage.

FOOD POISONING

- Rest! Food poisoning usually passes through your system in a couple days. Stay well hydrated, too, to help your body get rid of the bacteria.

- Carbonated drinks can help settle a queasy stomach, but take small sips and avoid anything too cold, which can be a shock to the system. Drinking sports drinks with electrolytes or sucking on ice chips also works.

- Stick to food that's easy on the stomach, like plain rice, soda crackers, bananas, cooked carrots, or oatmeal. Eat small quantities, and stop if the nausea returns. Avoid dairy products.

- If things get really serious, don't hesitate to call your doctor or go to the hospital. Some improperly cooked foods, like shellfish, can be extremely harmful.

GENERAL TIPS

- The number one thing to remember, regardless of what's ailing you, is *get enough rest*. Put everything but the most pressing deadlines on hold, slow down, take care of yourself, and don't make things worse.

- Find someone you can rely on to take care of you when you need it: your parents or roommate if you live with them, a nearby friend or family member if you live solo.

- As soon as you move into a new place, stock up on these basics: painkillers (acetaminophen for headaches, ibuprofen for muscle pain), gastrointestinal medication, vitamin C, hand sanitizer, a thermometer, a topical ointment for cuts, and bandages.

- Read all dosage information and do not exceed the recommended amount. Sign up for automatic prescription refills if your pharmacy offers them, and program a daily phone alarm to remind you to take your meds.

- Take antibiotics only if a doctor has prescribed them. Finish the full course, even if you feel better sooner; doing so will ensure the infection is treated completely. Don't drink alcohol while on antibiotics—you risk serious liver damage.

- Going to a real live doctor before your symptoms worsen is always a good idea. Trying to diagnose yourself with tools like WebMD is dicey and might just convince you that you're dying of some horrible disease (when in fact you just have the flu). Drop-in clinics (sometimes attached to a pharmacy) can address minor illnesses like strep throat, pink eye, and sinus infections.

- If you are experiencing severe pain or a high fever, can't keep down fluids, or have injured yourself, go to an emergency room.

How to Build a First Aid Kit

Every home in which a child lives needs a first-aid kit, and adult-only homes will greatly benefit too. Fortunately, they are easy to assemble and relatively inexpensive. Stock up on these essentials (and make sure to store out of the reach of any real or hypothetical children):

- Thermometer—oral is fine if you only associate with adults, but add a child-safe thermometer (digital, ear, or rectal) if children live with you or regularly visit

- Rubbing-alcohol swabs to clean the thermometer

- Petroleum jelly for lubrication if you have a rectal thermometer

- Acetaminophen or ibuprofen for pain and fevers, including child-safe dosages if there are children

- Saline nose drops, and/or nasal aspirator for toddlers and infants

- Topical calamine lotion to relieve insect bites and rashes

- Antibiotic ointment for cuts and bruises

- Adhesive bandages for cuts and bruises

- Gauze roll, gauze pads, and adhesive tape for larger cuts and bruises

- Tweezers and scissors

Medical Care 101

In an ideal world, every cut and cough would be treated promptly by an affordable medical provider. But in the real world, taking good care of yourself isn't easy to figure out—especially if you're already feeling woozy. (For more on insurance, see page 104.) Here's how to stay healthy, happy, and sane.

WHAT KIND OF DOCTOR DO I NEED?

- *General practitioners* (GPs) perform check-ups and treat illnesses in the beginning stages, referring patients to specialists if a problem progresses.

- *Gynecologists* deal broadly with the female reproductive organs, while *obstetricians* primarily handle childbirth and neonatal care. Many doctors work in both fields simultaneously (known as OB/GYNs).

- *Specialists* (podiatrists, dermatologists, allergists, etc.) concentrate on a specific body part or system. Your GP will refer you to one if needed.

- *Psychiatrists* diagnose and treat mental disorders and may specialize in one area, such as psychotherapy, eating disorders, or dementia-related problems. Unlike *therapists*, psychiatrists can prescribe medication.

- *Emergency room doctors and nurses* are responsible for triaging patients, assessing the problem, and beginning care. Once admitted to a hospital, a patient is usually sent to other doctors in appropriate departments, depending on the problem.

- *Walk-in clinicians*, whether doctors or nurse practitioners, work in facilities that accept patients without an appointment. Such clinics may focus on emergency care, immunization, or sexual health and often offer basic medical services only.

HOW DO I EVEN FIND A DOCTOR?

- Ask around for recommendations—friends and coworkers are more trustworthy than anonymous online reviews.

- Use an online search engine like ZocDoc, WebMD, or DocASAP to find doctors near your house or office.

- Browse your insurance company's internet portal for doctors guaranteed to be in-network.

- Find a doctor *before* you get sick. The last thing you want to do when you're ill is spend time researching practitioners.

WHEN DO I HAVE TO SEE MY DOCTOR?

- **Once a year for a checkup.** Preventative care is the easiest way to maintain good health. For some, that includes an annual gynecological exam and Pap smear. Some general practitioners will perform these; others will direct you to an OB/GYN.

- **At least once a year for teeth cleaning.** Nobody likes going to the dentist, but nobody likes root canals or gum surgery, either. Regular cleanings are the best prevention.

- **Every few months/partners if you're sexually active.** Clinics can handle Pap smears and urine tests (sometimes for free or at reduced cost for young people). If you're experiencing any symptoms, don't wait to get them checked.

- **If you're managing a chronic condition.** Visit your doctor more frequently if you have an ongoing condition like diabetes, heart problems, or chronic pain. Even if your treatment regimen is working, checking in is wise.

- **If you're dealing with mental health issues.** A psychiatrist will diagnose and treat problems like severe depression, anxiety, or mood disorders and can prescribe medication if appropriate.

- **After an accident.** Even if you feel fine! Everything from concussions to a broken toe can cause serious complications if not patched up properly.

- **For a severe allergic reaction.** If you experience hives, nausea/vomiting, shortness of breath, or swelling after contact with an allergen (food, medication, bug bite or sting, etc.), get to an emergency room *stat*!

- **If you're pregnant.** An obstetrician will make sure you're getting adequate nutrition and rest and monitor your baby's health, too.

How to Get Involved in a Cause

Volunteering to make the world a better place can help you meet new people, learn new skills, reduce stress, provide a sense of purpose, and even make you feel happier and healthier. Here's how to start.

1. **Make a list of what matters to you.** Think about the issues you are passionate about and the types of changes you want to see in your world. Your world can be defined in any way you want. It can be local, such as your town. It can be specific to a certain population. Or it can encompass larger issues that affect a broad region or multiple communities.

2. **Choose one thing that matters to you most.** Your time and resources are limited, and you can't fix every problem that exists. Choose one that feels extremely meaningful to you. It's likely that several of your issues are interconnected, but starting with one issue can provide you with a way to make meaningful change.

3. **Seek out people or organizations that share your beliefs.** Meaningful impact takes time and is likely to be achieved incrementally over a longer period through the collaborative work of individuals in support of larger organizations. Network locally to find others that share your passions. Speak with or write to politicians that share your values. Contact organizations that are dedicated to doing the work you care about.

4. **Contribute your time, energy, or money.** There are a number of ways to get involved, and to maximize your resources, you can pursue more than one, such as volunteering with one organization and donating money or goods to another.

   • **Volunteer.** Contact the organization and inquire about volunteer opportunities. Ask questions about the organization's mission to ensure it aligns with your values. Ask questions about the time commitment and any required training to make sure it fits your availability. Also, consider your skill set and what specific expertise you can offer the organization. For example, if you are a web developer, you can help update their website.

- **Donate.** Set aside a portion of your paycheck for contributions, or donate monthly if you can to support the mission year-round. If it's important for you to see your contribution in action, seek out local organizations that you can meet with about your donation.

- **Spread the word.** Use your excitement and passion to get others involved. Organize a fundraiser that introduces the organization to your friends or a volunteer day that encourages your coworkers to join in. If it's a national organization, perhaps there's a local fundraising event that you can get involved with or start on your own.

5. **Enjoy yourself.** The best experiences benefit you and the organization. If you find yourself no longer interested, reassess the situation and your involvement. The opportunity may no longer be a good fit for where you are in your life. Or maybe something has changed within the organization that no longer motivates you.

HOME
STUFF

How to Size Up an Apartment

Arrange to see the apartment you will be renting—not a model unit in the building or another property entirely. (Pro tip: Never sign for an apartment sight unseen!) Consider these factors.

- What's the 'hood like? An area with a bunch of settled families will be nice and quiet, but probably have fewer cool bars (and higher rent). A more up-and-coming part of town will be cheaper, but maybe not as safe.

- How close is it to work? Is there parking?

- How close are key amenities—grocery store, bus stop, Laundromat, doctor's office, park, decent pizza delivery? Be realistic about how far you're willing to travel.

- Is there room for your furniture? Will your stuff fit through the door/up the stairs?

- Are pets allowed?

- How much natural light comes into the space?

- Are the kitchen facilities adequate for your cooking habits?

- If you'll live with a partner or roommates, do they like the place, too? Remember, it'll be a looooong lease to ride out if anyone (including you) feels pushed into the living situation.

- Is everything in good, clean, working condition? Thoroughly check:

  - ○ Light fixtures

  - ○ Electrical sockets

  - ○ Taps and plumbing (it's not weird to give the toilet a test flush)

  - ○ Heating and air-conditioning

  - ○ Included appliances

  - ○ Storage space

  - ○ Locks

  - ○ Grout in kitchen and bathroom

  - ○ Cupboards/cupboard doors

  - ○ Smoke detectors

  - ○ Deadbolt locks, if the apartment opens onto a street

  - ○ Window bars, if you're on the first floor

  - ○ No mold, water damage, or weird smells

  - ○ No sign of insects or pests

- How long has the landlord had the property? Who does repairs? Get a name and phone number, and ask about past problems.

- When is rent due? How do you pay—cash or check, in person, by mail, or online?

- How soon can you get internet service?

- Who handles trash and recycling?

- Do you have access to common spaces—backyards, balconies, gym, storage rooms, bike racks? How are those monitored or shared?

- Can you receive packages? (Some buildings direct large deliveries to the nearest post office for pickup, which can be a real pain if you work during the day.)

- Why is the current/previous tenant moving? Ask for references from past or current renters of the unit or in the building. It's a red flag if a landlord isn't willing to share names.

READING AND SIGNING THE LEASE

In theory, a lease basically says "this person will pay this much for this apartment." In practice it's a little more complicated and may include rules and obligations that are easy to miss. Here's how to read the fine print.

- **Read the entire document.** Attentively. The lease should state the amount of rent you'll be paying, the date by which the rent must be paid (typically the first of every month), the appliances included in the rental, who is responsible for repairs, what happens if you violate the lease, and whether you're allowed to have pets, paint the walls, or hang things off your porch. Ask questions and raise concerns before you sign. All additions and amendments to the lease should be initialed by both parties.

- **Bring credentials.** Expect to have your credit history checked (usually for a charge, which shouldn't exceed $40 or so). Your landlord may also ask for proof of employment (pay stubs or employer contact info) and/or a letter of reference (especially for a fancier place). And it never hurts to bring photo ID.

- **To sign or co-sign?** Having your lease co-signed means that someone else will be legally responsible for the rent if you fall behind (which is handy if you don't have a steady paycheck or good credit history). Most first-time renters use their parents, who are usually comfortable with bearing such a legal responsibility for their offspring.

- **Pay up.** You'll typically have to pay the first and last month's rent and/or a security deposit (usually the amount of an additional month's rent) up front. Before you pay, ask how your landlord wants to be paid for these fees and for monthly rent (it may be different). Can they accept electronic payments? Do you need a specific app? If they need a check for your deposit, you can ask for one at your bank, or withdraw cash and purchase a money order at any bank or post office.

- **Know your commitment.** A one-year lease is typical. If you don't plan to stick around for the full term, ask ahead of time if the landlord will let you sublet (i.e., allow someone else to live in the space and pay rent, either to you or to the landlord). Also find out how much your landlord can legally raise the rent every year—in many places, around 5 percent is the norm.

How to Move

Moving is a total pain in the butt, but try to view it less as a really annoying chore and more as the perfect opportunity to streamline all your possessions. The following steps will make the process as painless as possible and help you lighten your load—literally.

- Make three piles—Keep, Donate, Trash—and start sorting. Now is not the time for sentimentality, so be realistic about how often you'll need that copy of Shakespeare's sonnets or those purple Mardi Gras beads.

- Don't put your bed (or other essentials) up for sale until a couple days before you move unless you have another place to sleep (or don't mind the floor).

- Got too much food? Throw a Let's Eat Everything in My Cupboards dinner party. Closet overflowing? Host a clothing swap party. Donate anything leftover to a local charity.

- Once you've pared down, it's time to pack. Most businesses (especially liquor stores) will hand over cardboard boxes if you ask nicely; in a pinch, hardware and big-box stores sell them for a moderate price. Pack clothes in luggage, rolling (not folding) garments to save space. Load soft items like linens in large garbage bags (double up in case of rips).

- Box things according to where they'll go in your new place, labeling the sides clearly so you and your friends/movers know where to put them.

- Carefully wrap breakable items like plates and cups, further protecting them with towels and bed sheets. Put soaps, shampoos, nail polishes, and other spillables in plastic bags.

- Distribute weight. Don't put an entire book-shelf's worth of books in one box—you won't be able to lift it. Fill it halfway, then pad out the rest with lighter items.

- You have a few vehicular options. Friends and their cars are wonderful if you ask nicely and supply pizza at the end of the day. A you-drive-it rental truck works if you can maneuver the vehicle and carry boxes yourself. Movers will take care of *everything* (sometimes even packing, though you'll want to supervise) but cost much more—investigate student mover companies for an affordable option. Don't rely on public transit or taxis unless you want to make a driver grumpy.

- Some stuff just won't survive the trip. Budget extra cash to replace things like cleaning supplies.

How to Complain to Your Landlord

The tenant/landlord relationship can be tricky. After all, you are relying on each other for basic needs like housing and income, and sometimes things go wrong.

Speaking up isn't necessarily *complaining*. The landlord's job is to fix problems, and you're passing along needed information. Be polite, respectful, and grateful when things are taken care of quickly. Here are some ways to keep communication flowing.

- **Be in touch.** An informal text message is an appropriate way to raise a complaint if your landlord is an individual rather than a company and you communicate mostly via texts. If you're dealing with a holdings company, think you may eventually have to take legal action, or simply feel the need for added gravitas, a formal letter is a better method. When drafting the letter, make sure it's polite and to the point. Include your name, address and unit number, the date, the problem, the solution you're expecting, and whatever portion of the lease agreement makes it the other party's responsibility. If you're *really* concerned, send it via registered mail.

- **Be timely.** The sooner your landlord knows about an issue, the faster it'll get fixed. Even if the repair is technically your responsibility, keep your landlord in the loop. It might be better to get a recommendation for a trusted tradesperson rather than tinker away at a door that won't close tight.

- **Be available.** Many landlords have spare keys and will work without you at home, but it's always a good idea to be on the premises when repairs happen, especially if outside contractors, like exterminators or plumbers, will be entering your home.

- **Brush up on legalese.** Google "tenant rights [your area]" and familiarize yourself with what you can and cannot expect from a landlord (many states have a downloadable tenant's handbook). Don't threaten to withhold rent until your unacceptable living situation improves, for example, unless you're sure you have the legal right to do so.

- **Implement a three-strike rule.** For conflicts between you and your neighbor with the penchant for wild Wednesday night parties, don't bring the landlord into the mix right away. Ask the neighbor to quiet down in person and *then* go to the landlord if nothing changes. "I've asked 4B three times not to leave cigarette butts everywhere, but they're not listening" is much easier to work with than a tenant who merely tattles.

How to Meal Plan and Grocery Shop

Think of a meal plan as a road map for food. Planning all the meals you'll eat for a week can save you a lot of money on pizza delivery (though, real talk, pizza is delicious). It'll also help you stop wasting food and avoid shopping five times a week. Here's how to get started.

- Draw a diagram (or use a day planner or even your smartphone calendar) with space for all the meals you'll eat.

- Next, look at your calendar and determine when you'll have time to shop and cook. If you're home only a few nights a week, plan to cook large meals that keep for several days (like stews and curries) and portion them out.

- Make healthy choices. Focus on fruits and vegetables (the darker the color, the more nutrient-rich the food) and whole grains, plus lean meats, fish, beans, eggs, and nuts for protein, dairy products for calcium, and as few saturated and trans fats as possible.

- Seek balance. Don't swear off junk food forever, but do try to offset Friday's pizza and beer with meals full of leafy greens on other days.

- Be realistic and flexible. You might not get home early enough to whip up that roast chicken, so stock up on quick meal options.

- Love your leftovers! Make double batches of recipes and freeze them for later (one-quart yogurt containers work great for storage). Pack a lunch-sized portion of dinner while you're washing up and the next day's midday meal is taken care of.

Based on your plan, make a shopping list, including any staples you're running low on. Having this list will make grocery shopping faster, less frequent, and clear of impulse purchases. Here are more tips for shopping smart.

- Seasonal produce is more affordable and hasn't been shipped halfway across the world. Shopping farmers' markets can also keep down costs, especially if you want to eat organic.

- Stock up on staples that don't spoil quickly. At the market, scoop as much rice, coffee, flour, and other dry goods as you need; at a big-box discounter, grab massive quantities of things like paper towels and toothpaste. Just make sure you can store (and carry!) everything you buy.

- Smaller markets, bodegas, or convenience stores are just that—convenient, and often more expensive. Then again, some mom-and-pop grocery stores are treasure troves of good deals on nonperishables, so check prices!

- Forget coupons. Many chain groceries now have smartphone apps that let you collect points and cash in on deals.

- "Shortcut" foods like cooked chicken strips and grated cheese are convenient but often more expensive. Weigh time vs. money carefully!

Basic Cooking Techniques

You've decided what you'll be eating and stocked the necessary ingredients. Time to get cooking!

- **Making a basic vinaigrette:** In the bottom of a large bowl (big enough to fit all the salad ingredients), add 1 tablespoon of red wine vinegar, 4 tablespoons of olive oil, and a pinch each of salt and pepper. Whisk together (you can use a fork!). Optional additions: herbs (like rosemary), a dollop of grainy mustard, or a squeeze of lemon juice.

- **Boiling the perfect hard-cooked egg:** Place eggs in a large saucepan and add enough cool water to cover by 1 inch. Over medium heat, bring the water to a steady boil, then remove the pan from the heat, cover, and let it sit for 12 minutes. Prepare an ice bath (ice cubes and water in a small bowl). Drain eggs in a colander and dunk them in the ice bath to stop cooking and cool them. Then dry, peel, and enjoy.

- **Tear-free onion cutting:** With a sharp knife, cut the onion in half, then peel off the skin and lay each half flat side down on a cutting board. Cut off the stem (but not the roots—they'll hold the layers in place), and make cuts perpendicular to the root about ¼ inch apart. Turn each half 90 degrees and cut again, perpendicular to your first cuts, resulting in perfect(ish) little cubes.

- **Seasoning *everything*:** Herbs and spices are an important part of what makes food taste good. Everyone's palate is different, so don't be afraid to experiment—though the myriad choices can overwhelm the inexperienced cook. Just remember: practice makes perfect. Note that dried herbs have a more concentrated flavor than fresh herbs, so if you substitute fresh for dried in a recipe, you will need about three times as much to achieve the same flavor.

- **Thawing frozen meat:** The safest way is to defrost it in the fridge overnight. If you're in a hurry, remove the meat from its package, put it on a plate, and run it under cool water in the sink. The microwave should be a last resort—you might accidentally start cooking it! Always cook meat to the proper temperature: 165°F (74°C) for poultry, 160°F (71°C) for ground meats, 145°F (63°C) for steaks, pork, and fish.

- **Cooking rice:** In a medium saucepan, bring 1½ cups of water to a boil. Stir in 1 cup of long-grain white rice (basmati, for example) and ½ teaspoon of salt. Reduce heat to medium-high and bring to a boil, then reduce to low, cover the pan, and cook for 16–18 minutes, until the rice is tender and has absorbed the water (you'll see little holes made by the steam when it's ready). Remove from heat and leave covered for 10 minutes, then fluff rice with a fork.

- **Steaming vegetables:** Clean and peel the vegetables and cut them into uniform bite-sized chunks. Add 1 inch of water to a saucepan equipped with a steamer basket. Put veggie pieces in the steamer basket, ensuring they're not touching the water. Bring water to a boil over high heat, then reduce heat to medium and cover. After a few minutes, poke the thickest part of the vegetables with a fork to see if they're tender. Remove from the heat while they're still a bit crunchy—they'll keep cooking and be perfect by the time they're eaten. If you're cooking different veggies together, remember that denser ones, like carrots or potatoes, cook more slowly than the likes of mushrooms or peppers, so add longer-cooking items to the steamer first and then wait a while to add the quicker-cooking vegetables.

NECESSARY EQUIPMENT FOR EVERY KITCHEN

- ❍ Sharp knives (8- or 9-inch chef's knife, paring knife, and serrated knife)
- ❍ Spatula
- ❍ Ladle
- ❍ Tongs
- ❍ Wooden spoon
- ❍ Cutting board
- ❍ Pots (one big and one small, with lids)
- ❍ Nonstick frying pan or wok
- ❍ Mixing bowls
- ❍ Measuring cups and spoons
- ❍ Rimmed baking sheet
- ❍ Grater
- ❍ Strainer or colander
- ❍ Pyrex or ceramic baking dishes
- ❍ Muffin tins, cake pans, pie tins, and other specialty bakeware
- ❍ Handheld electric mixer

How to Sew a Hem

Even if you don't know the first thing about sewing, you can learn to sew a basic hem, which will save you an unnecessary trip to the tailor.

1. Thread a sewing needle with approximately two feet of thread. Knot the two ends of the thread together near the bottom.

2. Turn the garment inside out, with the hem facing you.

3. Firmly attach the knotted end of the thread by making one or two stitches on the underside of the garment (so the thread won't show when you're wearing it).

4. Make a hem stitch (see illustration on page 59) by pushing the needle from the underside of the garment to the front, keeping in mind that the stitches should show as little as possible on the front of the garment. Repeat along the length of the hem.

5. If the material is heavy, just pick up some of the threads with the needle; don't go all the way through to the front. For thin fabrics, catching

only one thread is necessary (really!). Don't pull your stitches too tight; a hem stitch should look like a loose zigzag.

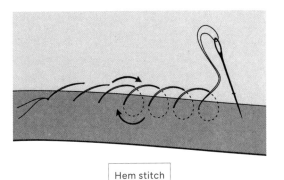

Hem stitch

Shortcut: Never underestimate the power of hem tape. You'd be amazed at how many things you can achieve with an iron (you do know how to iron, right? If not, see page 66) and some hem tape, no sewing necessary. Pants too long? Hem tape. Shortening curtains? Hem tape. Anything that needs to be stuck together in a straight line can be done quickly and easily with hem tape. And it's cheap, too. You can find hem tape in craft stores or online. Just fold a hem, put the tape inside the fold, and iron—the heat melts the tape into a glue that will withstand normal washing and wear.

OTHER SEWING TECHNIQUES

Here's how to quickly mend other minor sartorial emergencies that always pop up at inopportune moments.

- **Fixing a ripped seam:** Turn the garment inside out and lay it flat. Before starting to sew, you may want to hold the fabric in place with a few pins. Then sew the ripped section along the crease of the original seam using small backstitches: after your first stitch forward, backtrack half a stitch from where you started, go forward and backtrack again half the new stitch, then forward again. (See illustration on page 61.) This will make the fabric react as if it were sewn on a machine, which is necessary because sewing in a straight line will make the fabric fall and stretch differently in that one section than in the rest of the seam.

- **Fixing those strange little frayed-at-the-edges holes in jackets and T-shirts:** Use thread that matches the clothing's color as closely as possible, opting for a shade slightly darker rather than lighter. Thread the needle and knot the ends. Sew from the back of the garment so

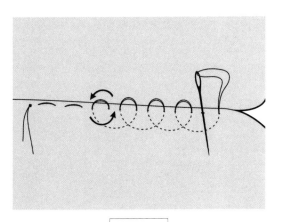

Backstitch

that the knot and stitches are hidden. If you're working with knits or jersey, be sure to catch an intact stitch on all sides of the hole. Secure your handiwork with small backstitches and finish by bringing your needle once or twice through the loop created between thread and fabric.

- **Fixing loose lining in a coat or jacket:** Thread your needle and make a few small stitches in the fabric to secure it. Knot the end of the ripped thread to your new thread to prevent further unraveling. Sew inside the crease of the folded underlining using small stitches. When finished, knot your thread and the loose thread at the other end of the former rip.

- **Adding a patch:** If you're not dealing with an immediate emergency, and you have a little more time to fix your rip or hole, you may want to reinforce the area with a patch. Patches are especially good for holes that come from wear or friction, like the ones that arise on the elbows of jackets or the inner thighs of jeans. Cut a piece of fabric about an inch larger than the hole on all sides, place it inside the garment, and sew around it with a backstitch (see page 61). Or head to the craft store for iron-on patches, no sewing required!

How to Sew On a Button

Tailors and dry cleaners can replace buttons inexpensively, but for the flat kind on most shirts and jackets, it's easy (and cheaper) to do it yourself.

1. Select a button and thread that match the article of clothing. Thread that is slightly darker than the fabric is ideal, because the stitches will blend better (lighter thread stands out more).

2. Thread a needle so that there is 1 foot (30 cm) of thread on both sides of the needle. If you have trouble, lick the end of the thread before inserting it through the needle's eye.

3. Knot the two ends of the thread together.

4. Position the button on the fabric, making sure that it is aligned with the corresponding buttonhole as well as the other buttons on the garment.

5. Starting from the underside of the fabric, push the needle through the fabric and one hole of the button. Pull the thread all the way through.

6. Push the needle down through the next hole in the button and through the fabric, pulling the thread all the way through.

7. Bring the needle back through the fabric and a hole in the button, and repeat this process about ten times to ensure that the button will stay put (Figure A).

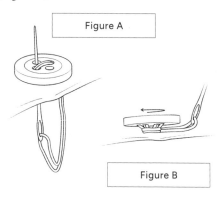

Figure A

Figure B

8. Then pull the needle and thread through the fabric under the button, but not through a hole. Pull the thread all the way through. Wrap it around the thread that holds the button to the fabric three or four times (Figure B).

9. Push the needle back through to the underside of the fabric and pull it taut. Angling the needle almost flat against the fabric, push it through the fabric but not to the surface (Figure C).

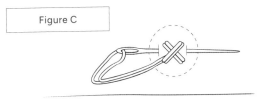

Figure C

10. Before you pull the thread taut, pull the needle through the loop in the thread a few times to create a knot. Repeat several times, overlaying stitches to secure the knot (Figure D).

Figure D

11. Trim excess thread.

Tip: Place a penny under the edge of the button while you sew to ensure there is enough slack for the button to be pulled through its corresponding buttonhole and accommodate the additional layer of fabric.

How to Iron

If you plan to iron more than the occasional blouse, invest in a good-quality ironing board and an iron that has a steam setting and self-cleaning feature. Always remember: you can iron something nicely only if it's laid flat.

- Familiarize yourself with the iron's settings; fabrics need varying levels of heat. (Don't iron silk or a synthetic on the wool setting or you'll have a puckered, melted mess!)

- Fill the water reservoir if you plan to use steam.

- Read the care instructions on any garment you plan to iron. If there are none, try to determine the fabric and select that setting. When in doubt, always start on a cooler setting and test the temperature on a less obvious spot before ironing the entire garment.

- Acrylics may stick to a hot iron; velvets may become permanently shiny. To avoid mishaps, turn the garment inside out or place a clean cotton cloth, or press sheet, between the garment and the iron.

- Make sure no fabric is bunched up under the area you're ironing.

- For best results on cotton, iron when the fabric is still a bit damp. If it's completely dry, mist it with water, roll it up loosely, and let it sit for a minute before ironing.

- Move the iron slowly, being careful not to leave it in one place (unless you want an iron-shaped scorch mark there). Spray stubborn wrinkles with water and iron in a figure-eight motion.

- When ironing collared shirts, you'll have a much easier time if you use a sleeve board. Fold the sleeves in half vertically and iron down the middle from both sides, avoiding the fold so that you don't iron in a crease. Pull the sleeves over the sleeve board and iron. Then do the back, the sides, and the front, using the tip of the iron to reach between the buttons. Lay the collar flat and iron it on both sides. Avoid ironing it down, which will make it look flat. Fold the collar and bend it over your knee to give it a curved shape.

How to Hold a Baby

Whether you're preparing for parenthood or just friends with parents of a newborn, you should be comfortable holding a baby. And it's good to know how to do that before you are thrust into the moment. So be prepared and try the simple "cradle hold" (Figure A).

1. Place the baby's head in the crook of your arm (the inside bend of the elbow).

2. Secure the baby's body with that hand.

3. Use your free arm for support as necessary.

4. To calm a fussy baby, rock your arms gently back and forth.

Figure A

And if you really want to show off, hold the baby in the "potato sack" carry (Figure B).

1. Position yourself behind a baby in the facedown position.

2. Slide your dominant hand between the baby's legs, resting it palm up on the baby's chest.

3. Use your other hand to secure the baby.

4. Scoop up the baby and carry at your side, as if holding a football.

Figure B

For older babies who have greater head and neck control, the hip hold is also recommended (Figure C).

1. Rest the baby's bottom on your hip, with their chest resting against your side.

2. Wrap that same arm around the baby's bottom and lower back.

Figure C

Another option for older babies is to hold them so that they can see what is going on—the "faceout hold" (Figure D).

1. Support the baby's back by placing it against your chest so that the baby is facing forward.

2. Place one arm under the baby's bottom.

3. Place the other arm across the baby's chest.

Figure D

How to Bottle-Feed a Baby

So you need to feed a baby, but for whatever reason, you're not feeding it out of your personal body. That means you'll be using a bottle. Here's how you make sure it's well received.

1. If you're using formula, prepare it according to the package directions. Let's repeat that: *read the directions.* Not all formulas are identical. If you're using refrigerated or frozen breast milk, warm it under running water, starting cool and gradually increasing the heat. *Or* do whatever the owner of the baby tells you to do.

2. If you'd like to bring the bottle to room temperature, run it under warm water for a minute or two. Do *not* heat the bottle in the microwave.

3. Sit down. Position the baby in the "cradle hold" position (see page 68) with their head in the crook of your arm and raised slightly above the rest of their body. For comfort, you may want to rest your arm or the baby's bottom on your lap.

4. Fasten a bib around the baby's neck to prevent soiling or wetting their clothing.

5. Place the bottle upside down or in a position that fills the nipple with formula.

6. Gently position the nipple inside the baby's mouth. Their reflex should kick in, and they will start sucking.

7. Remove the bottle after five or ten minutes or if feeding has stalled.

8. Put a cloth on your shoulder and hold the baby against your chest, with their head near your shoulder, facing behind you. Pat gently on the baby's back until they burp.

9. Continue feeding until the baby is full or the bottle is empty. Each baby will eat a different amount; there's no true standard. If it's your baby, and you think they're consistently not eating enough, consult your pediatrician. (If it's not your baby, butt out.)

How to Change a Diaper

If you have your own baby, you'll have to get used to this. (Don't worry, the first time is the hardest.) If you're pitching in for a friend or relative, they're gonna owe you big time. So buck up, rip off the tabs, and follow these instructions to get in and out as efficiently as possible.

1. Gather all the items you need: child, fresh diaper, baby wipes.

2. Lay the baby faceup on either a changing table or a changing pad arranged on the floor. If using a changing table, make certain to fasten the safety straps. You may prefer a changing pad on the floor because it's safer and easier to position yourself in front of the baby.

3. Place the fresh, open diaper under the baby's still-dirty-diapered bottom with the tabs on the portion that is under the baby's bottom. Doing this now provides an additional layer between the mess and whatever surface you're using, which is important since it will need to be cleaned at the end.

4. Unfasten the diaper tabs and use one hand to lift the baby's ankles so that their bottom is raised slightly above the dirty diaper. You may want to strategically place a baby wipe to avoid being sprayed by an accidental urination.

5. Clean the messy area with baby wipes. Always wipe from front to back, especially when wiping a baby girl.

6. Once clean, apply any recommended lotions or ointments.

7. Close the diaper by folding up the front section and opening and securing the sticky tabs. Do not make the diaper too tight or leave it too loose. You should be able to slide one or two fingers between the baby's belly and the diaper.

8. Dispose of the messy diaper and wipes in a diaper pail. Wash your hands and the changing area.

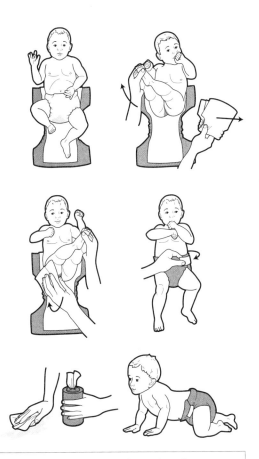

Being organized is the key to diaper-changing success.

How to Change a Tire

This minor emergency is bound to befall you sooner or later, so be prepared. Know the necessary steps before it happens, and you'll save yourself a lot of stress.

1. As soon as you notice you have a flat, stop driving. Pull over onto a smooth concrete area with no slope and engage the emergency brake.

2. Most cars are equipped with a spare tire, jack, and lug wrench (the manual will tell you where to find them, but typically they're in the trunk). Carefully read the directions before using these items. Two things you won't find next to the lug wrench but will be glad you kept there: a blanket to put between your new jeans and a dirty highway, and some heavy gloves to protect your hands from grease.

3. While the tire is still on the ground, use your lug wrench to loosen the lugs (the bolts that keep your tires in place) just a little. That will make removing them easier once the car is jacked (raised off the ground). Think *righty tighty, lefty loosey*: attach the lug wrench in the direction you want to turn it, parallel to the ground, and turn

the wrench to loosen the lugs. You may need to use your foot to push down and loosen the lugs.

Turn the wrench to loosen the lugs.

4. Refer to the car's manual to determine the right spot at which to jack up your car. There is usually a little notch or lip in the side of the car where the jack should go. Jack up the car.

5. Completely unscrew the loosened lug nuts and remove the flat tire.

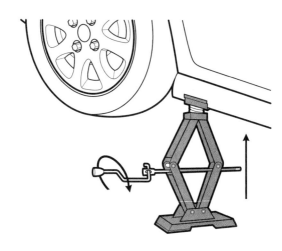

Be sure to jack up your car at the right spot.

6. Line up the spare with your lug bolts and push it in as far as you can. Because the tire won't simply rest flush on the bolts by itself, you'll need to hold it in place to properly screw on the nuts.

7. Now begin to replace the lug nuts. Screw them on with your hands as much as possible; then grab your lug wrench and tighten as much as you can. Always tighten nuts across from each other rather than going around in a circle, and never

pull up when tightening—go with gravity and push down.

8. Lower your jack stand and finish tightening your lug nuts using your foot (see step 3). You want them to be as tight as possible.

9. Spares aren't made to be driven on for long. Put your tools and flat tire in the trunk and drive to the closest gas station. If the tire isn't too damaged, the mechanic may be able to plug it; otherwise you'll need to replace it.

How to Check Your Oil

Oil is necessary for the proper function of your vehicle; it lubricates and reduces friction in the motor. Without enough oil, your engine can seize up, effectively ruining your car. You should change the oil as often as the car manufacturer recommends (usually between 5,000 and 7,500 miles). And make sure you're using the proper type for your car. Follow these steps to check and adjust the oil level.

1. For a proper reading, park the car on level ground and turn off the engine. Have a rag handy that you're okay staining with oil.

2. Pop the hood and locate the dipstick, which will be close to the front of the engine. (Consult the owner's manual if you can't locate it.) Pull it out and wipe it clean with the rag.

3. Reinsert the clean dipstick all the way. Remove it again, making sure to keep it pointing down. Do not turn it upside down, because any oil trickling upward will throw off the reading.

4. Hold the dipstick diagonally pointing down, and support the tip with your rag. Look for two lines etched at the bottom of the dipstick.

Ideally your oil level will be between those lines. Depending on your vehicle, the low level may be marked with the word "low" or "add," instead of lines (see illustration on page 82).

5. If your oil level is above the top line, you need some removed and probably need an oil change. Over-oiling causes oil to foam and can damage engine components.

6. If your oil level is below the bottom line, add a little. Unscrew the oil cap on the top of your engine (look for the oil symbol, which resembles a genie's lamp). Using a funnel, pour in half a quart of oil, taking care not to overfill. Start the car, and go for a short drive. Then check the oil again and see if you need more. If you do, add another ¼ quart.

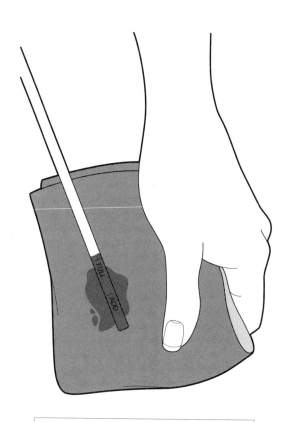

The oil level should be between the two
etched lines at the bottom of the dipstick.

How to Jump-Start a Car

A dead battery is an easy thing to fix—provided that you've got a set of jumper cables in the trunk. (Put a set of jumper cables in your trunk!)

1. Refer to your car's owner's manual. It may provide important information on the particulars of your specific car. Some models require you to use special lugs designed for jump-starting, instead of connecting directly to the battery.

2. Recruit a driver with a working automobile. Park their working automobile beside your car so that the two batteries are as close as possible. Be sure the two cars are not touching each other.

3. Put both cars in park with the emergency brake engaged. Turn the cars off.

4. Pop the hoods of both cars.

5. Attach the red-handled (positive) clamp at one end of the jumper cable to the positive terminal on the dead battery.

6. Attach the red-handled (positive) jumper cable clamp at the other end to the positive terminal on the fully charged battery.

7. Attach the black-handled (negative) clamp at the first end of the jumper cable to the negative terminal on the charged battery.

8. Ground the remaining black-handled (negative) jumper cable clamp to an exposed piece of clean metal on the dead car's engine—usually a nice shiny bolt will do the trick.

9. Start the working automobile, and allow it to run for 2 to 3 minutes.

10. Start the car with the dead battery. If the engine starts, wait 3 or 4 minutes, and then remove the clamps one at a time in reverse order. Allow the "jumped" car to run for at least 30 minutes before turning it off, to ensure that the battery is fully charged.

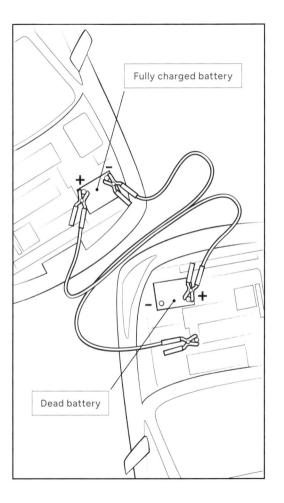

Fully charged battery

Dead battery

WORK AND MONEY STUFF

How to Write a Résumé and Cover Letter

A résumé is the document with all the information—previous jobs, education, skills—that a prospective employer will need to determine that you are, of course, the best candidate for the job. It's like a cheat sheet for your awesomeness. Here's how to write a standout.

- Put contact information at the top. (You want your new boss to be able to reach you with the good news!) Share as many details and links as you're comfortable with, including your personal website or social media, if relevant/applicable.

- Keep your employment history brief; include only information relevant to the job you're applying for (spare your prospective employer from reading about your high-school snack-bar job), and limit job descriptions to one or two sentences.

- A section about your skills can include anything from the languages you speak to the equipment you know how to operate—it depends on the job. If you're struggling to think of pertinent items—or how to phrase them—search for job postings in your field and see what they say an ideal candidate should be able to do. If you can do those things, list them.

- Extra information like your hobbies, athletic awards, or volunteer experience isn't mandatory but can set you apart from the crowd (you never know, you could bond with your interviewer over a mutual love of Latin). Add what you think is best.

Where a résumé outlines your background and experience, the cover letter is an opportunity to tailor that information to the position you're applying for—adding context—and it's often the first thing a prospective employer will read. No pressure, right? Here's how to rock it.

- Write clearly, concisely, and professionally. Even relaxed informal companies will want a cover letter that is serious and demonstrates your communication skills. Sound like yourself, but your sharpest, smartest self.

- Why do you want the job? (No, "I'm broke" doesn't count.) Why are you the best person for the position? Explain how your previous work applies to this job or why your skills are a perfect fit.

- Even if you're seeking employment in a creative field, keep the cover letter simple and legible. Use a black, basic font in 12-point type, and do not exceed one page (or three medium-sized paragraphs if it's an email letter).

- Read application requirements thoroughly, and answer questions to the best of your ability. Some people may want the cover letter sent as the body of an email, rather than an attachment, or formatted in a particular way. Some postings will ask that you direct your application to a specific human resources contact. Proofread everything—don't lose points for something as trivial as misspelling a name.

- Also mention: where you heard about the job, how you first learned about the organization, mutual connections. (If you know a current or former employee, name them! Just make sure to get their approval first.)

- Dream company isn't hiring? You can still send a cover letter to introduce yourself as a possible employee. All the same rules apply: discuss why you're a good fit for the work and the company, and show off your experience and achievements.

How to Nail an Interview

Congratulations! All that time spent polishing your cover letter and choosing just the right font for your résumé paid off. Now you just need to meet face-to-face with whoever will be deciding your future—totally *not* terrifying. Prepare with these tips, and all will go smoothly.

BEFORE

- Get the basic information. Know when and where the interview will be taking place, plus any door codes or sign-in instructions you'll need. Ask if the interviewer would like you to bring anything in particular and whether a test will be administered.

- Be on time. Scratch that—be early. Plan your travel route and arrange backup transportation. Be sure you know where in the building you're headed so you don't end up wandering around.

- Virtual interview? Test your internet connection, camera, and microphone ahead of time. (Also, it doesn't hurt to make sure your computer camera is pointed toward your most impressive books.)

- Learn the organization's history and goals. Google-stalk the founder. Read interviews and press releases. Show that you are informed and care about the people you're hoping to work for.

- Prepare answers for the following questions:

  ○ Why you are interested in the job

  ○ Why you are interested in the organization

  ○ What your strengths and weaknesses are

  ○ What you hope to learn

  ○ What your previous experiences bring to this job

  ○ Why you are the best candidate

  ○ When you can start/what your schedule is like

  ○ What the organization does well/what they could be doing better

- Have questions of your own (and no, "when can I start?" doesn't count). It shows that you've put thought into the position and are interested in learning more. Some potential questions:

  ○ Whom will I be reporting to/whom will I be working closely with?

  ○ What are the day-to-day responsibilities? What's a typical workday like?

- ❍ What qualities are you looking for in a candidate?

- ❍ Is there opportunity for growth within the organization?

- ❍ If I wish to learn new skills, is the organization interested in fostering that?

- ❍ Is there anything I can do to make myself a more attractive candidate?

- Wear appropriate, neat, clean, professional clothing even if the office is casual. Don't arrive listening to music, drinking coffee, or chewing gum (although a breath mint beforehand is probably a good idea).

DURING

- Bring all relevant materials. Better yet, bring *all* materials, relevant or otherwise: copies of your résumé and cover letter, work samples, personal business cards and a portfolio if you have them.

- Give a good handshake. Make eye contact and smile, then extend your arm and grasp the interviewer's hand firmly. You don't want to squeeze the person's hand painfully, but a weak, floppy grip is no good either. Shake from the elbow, once, maybe twice.

- Sit upright during the entire interview. You don't want to look like you're about to run away, but now is not the time to kick back and slump in the chair.

- Take time if you need to think up a good response. Repeat after me: "That's a great question, I hadn't considered it before." If you still can't think of something, it's okay to say "I don't know, but I'd hope to learn."

- *Slooooow down.* Remember to breathe. Try to avoid saying "like" and "um" or ending your sentences like a question? And relax, because you're doing great.

AFTER

- Let your interviewer know that you appreciate their time—a handwritten note is never too much! Reiterate how excited you are about the job ("I really enjoyed learning more about your company and the opportunity you're offering"), answer any questions you might not have been able to respond to during the interview ("You had asked me about my web design skills, and I thought you might like to know that . . ."), and offer to send supplementary material ("I'm happy to provide additional references or work samples").

- Don't write about the interview or job online! Even if you have nothing but good things to say, keep it to yourself. You can always jubilantly take to social media *after* you've secured the position.

- If you don't hear back within a few weeks, send a polite follow-up email. It doesn't have to be elaborate, just a quick word letting them know you're still interested and thinking about the job. You want to keep reminding whoever is making the decision that you exist.

- If you don't get the job, be gracious and don't burn bridges. Thank them for considering you, express that you'd love if they kept you in mind for future openings, and wish them the best with their new employee.

How to Ask for a Raise

You've put in your time and worked your butt off, and now you deserve a raise. Good for you! So, what's the best way to get one? Read on.

1. First of all, try to be objective and realistic when determining whether you've earned a raise. Don't go by what your friends tell you. And whatever you do, don't say you *need* a raise. That implies you're asking for one because you can't pay your bills, not because your work merits more compensation.

2. When you start a job, it's a good idea to ask how salary increases are handled. If you didn't, check your company's policy on raises. If there's a formal policy or review, wait until you've reached the benchmark before starting the conversation.

3. Itemize your responsibilities as you understand them or as they were presented to you. Describe how you have performed your tasks and define your accomplishments. If your company conducts formal evaluations, refer to those as a guideline—but don't cite them verbatim. If there is no formal review policy, try to remember

positive comments your managers have made about your work. Again, use them as a guideline, but don't quote them exactly.

4. Set up a meeting with your manager for the sole purpose of discussing your pay level. Give sufficient notice; don't just wander in. Try to do so when you know your manager is in a positive mood.

5. Practice, practice, practice. Rehearse as you would for any presentation. Try to treat it as though you're arguing the case for someone else instead of yourself—it's best to stay unemotional when the topic is money.

6. At the meeting, make your case as you rehearsed it. Don't be intimidated by your manager's reaction or comportment. You're prepared for this, remember? Be upbeat and positive, not nervous or defensive.

7. Don't bring up what your friends earn for similar jobs. The last thing you want to hear is, "Then go work for that company." (However, you may want to research salary trends for your industry and region, to have an idea of what someone

doing your job makes at other similar companies. This will put your request in context and help you gauge an appropriate increase to ask for.)

Note: Common sense dictates that if your company is struggling financially, it's best to hold off on your salary-hike request. However, do make sure that management is aware that's why you're waiting. Tell your boss that you believe you've earned a raise but will wait until things look brighter. You'll appear as both a team player and a savvy employee aware of their worth. Well played.

How to Deal with Taxes

No one likes paying taxes. No one. Welcome to adulthood! But they do have to be paid, and if you're organized and informed, the task won't seem so daunting (and you might even save some money).

WASN'T MY INCOME ALREADY TAXED?

Yes, but the amount withheld from your paycheck is essentially a prepayment on the tax you owe the government. Once you've filed your taxes, it'll become clear if you've either over- or underpaid; if it's the former, you'll be getting a refund. Yay!

WHEN DO I FILE?

The federal filing deadline in the United States is April 15 (e.g., the deadline for tax year 2025 is April 15, 2026), but you can file as soon as you have the appropriate paperwork from your employer(s). File as early as you can—your nerves will thank you! If you work freelance or are self-employed, you may need to file taxes once a quarter. Check with your city and state revenue service.

DO I HAVE TO FILE?

In short: yes. If you made any money, you absolutely need to *file* your taxes, even if you might not be able to *pay* them. Otherwise, the government will fine you for both failing to file and failing to pay and will charge interest for every month you're late. You will end up paying, it's just a question of how much.

BUT I'M UNEMPLOYED/I STILL LIVE WITH MY PARENTS!

Even if you're currently camped out in your parents' house watching *The Last Unicorn* for the nineteenth time, you still have to file your taxes. You might think it's useless (or hugely unfair) to be on the hook for tax filing when you're unemployed, but you still have to (particularly if you've been collecting unemployment benefits, which are considered income). You can, however, deduct the costs of looking for work, including travel costs and similar job-seeking expenses.

WHAT PAPERWORK DO I NEED?

If you have a salaried job (i.e., a job where your employer withholds taxes from each paycheck), you should receive a W-2 form from your employer detailing important info like your salary, taxes withheld, and employer ID number. If you do independent contractor work, you should have a form 1099-MISC from every company that has paid you more than $600 in the year. You'll use these forms to fill out a federal form 1040, 1040-EZ (if you have no dependents), or 1040-ES (if you're paying estimated taxes on non-withheld payments; see above). You can download the forms from irs.gov or file electronically.

If you're working freelance, congratulations, you're self-employed! Unless you've incorporated yourself, your business is considered a sole proprietorship and, along with your regular 1040 form, you'll need to file a Schedule C (though if your company is just you, you may be eligible to use the simplified Schedule C-EZ). If your net profit for the year exceeded the IRS's cutoff, you'll also need to file for self-employment tax (which means you're filing as employee *and* employer) using Schedule SE.

Additionally, if you plan to claim any deductions (see below), you'll need to keep receipts all year as proof of what you spent your money on. (Making a spreadsheet of monthly expenses can be helpful, but at the least keep hard copies in an envelope somewhere.)

AM I A DEPENDENT OR NOT?

In the United States, you are considered someone's dependent if you are a relative or child who lived in their home for the entire year; received more than 50 percent of your support from them; are a US citizen, national, or resident alien; and earned less than a certain amount that year (usually in the $4,000–$5,000 range). If these things apply, the person in question may claim you as a dependent and qualify for an exemption. You may still be asked to file your own taxes, though, and you don't get an exemption for *being* someone's dependent.

DO I GET ANY EXEMPTIONS, DEDUCTIONS, OR CREDITS?

Maybe. *Exemptions* are amounts you can automatically subtract from your income based on things like where you live and your marital status. *Deductions* are expenses such as student loans and charitable donations that the government won't tax. *Credits* are amounts taken out of the tax you owe; if you attended school in the past year, have a dependent child, or have a retirement plan, for example, you can take advantage of associated credits. As for deductions, check the "standard deduction" for your tax year; if your total deductions are less than that amount, you can claim the standard deduction and don't have to itemize (i.e., make a list of) all your deductions.

DO I HAVE TO WRITE AN ACTUAL PAPER CHECK?

It's the twenty-first century, and you can file your taxes using software designed for that purpose! Government websites will often list approved programs—some with free versions. Sign up for a direct deposit option, if it's available, so that your refund goes directly into your bank account. No matter how you file, make and keep hard copies of all forms.

THERE'S STILL SOMETHING I DON'T GET . . .

If you can afford to, hire an accountant. Otherwise, take to the internet. Also look up tax advice that is specific to your industry—there might be tips you hadn't considered. And check whether your income qualifies you for the Volunteer Income Tax Assistance program. They'll help you with your taxes for free. (Also, don't forget that it's fully legal to call the IRS for help! No one will yell at you!)

How to Deal with Insurance

Insurance in a nutshell: you pay a regular fee, or *premium*, to an organization that agrees to pay for damages in case of an accident or theft. If that happens, you'll file a *claim*, usually a list of damages or stolen items, sometimes accompanied by photos. Here's a breakdown of the types of insurance you might need.

HEALTH INSURANCE

Health insurance comes from one of three places: your job, the government, or a plan you purchase as an individual. Your employment and financial situations will dictate which is the best choice for you. Several types of plans exist:

- **Exclusive provider organization (EPO):** a plan in which services are covered only if you use doctors and facilities in the plan's network. (Emergency situations are the exception.)

- **Health maintenance organization (HMO):** Similarly to EPOs, an HMO will likely cover care only from doctors who work with it. You may be required to live or work in the HMO's service area, and the focus is often on preventative care.

- **Point of service (POS):** A POS will provide you with a list of primary physicians whom you have to visit in order to be referred to other doctors (often specialists). You have the option of seeing doctors outside the POS network, but you'll pay more out of pocket.

- **Preferred provider organization (PPO):** A PPO gives you the choice of visiting doctors both in and out of the network. You will pay more if you choose to go outside the network, but you don't need a referral from your primary care doctor.

No matter how invincible you feel, having health insurance is a good idea. If you're under the age of twenty-six, you may qualify for coverage under your parents' insurance. If you're a US citizen, you can sign up for a plan through the federal health insurance marketplace at healthcare.gov, but only during the time of year designated as an "open enrollment period."

CAR INSURANCE

If you own a car, you must have *liability insurance*— it's legally required almost everywhere in the US and Canada. This type of auto insurance covers anything you as a driver are liable for after an accident, like medical bills and property damage.

If you want insurance to cover repairs to your car after an accident, you'll want *collision coverage*—not legally required and perhaps not worth it if your car is older.

Comprehensive coverage will cover damage done to your car from things other than collisions, like weather mishaps, one-car accidents (like if you hit a deer), and theft.

Personal injury protection will pay for medical bills for you and your passengers, regardless of who was at fault in an accident.

Young people tend to pay a higher auto premium, but you can minimize costs by driving safely (more accidents = riskier to insure = more $$) and driving a "safe" car (i.e., a gently used sedan instead of a flashy new convertible).

RENTER'S INSURANCE

Renter's, or tenant's, insurance covers loss of possessions to fire, flood, or theft. It can also cover things like hotel stays if your landlord decides to fumigate the building.

Though often required by the terms of a lease, renter's insurance is a good idea regardless: an average payment of $17 a month will get you around $30,000 worth of coverage.

Pay close attention to what your policy includes; things like earthquakes aren't always covered. Keep an inventory list of everything you own to make filing claims go smoothly.

POSSESSION INSURANCE

Expensive items that could be stolen or damaged are often insured individually, since renter's insurance coverage caps how much you can claim for individual objects.

If you have your great-grandma's diamond necklace lying around, by all means insure it, but also consider expensive items that you need for work—power tools, musical instruments, electronics, etc.

Other Types of Insurance: Shelling out for things like life insurance, travel insurance, and pet insurance might seem smart, but resist the urge to overbuy. Unless you have dependents, for example, you probably don't need life insurance. Not sure? Make a pros and cons list to see if it's worth budgeting for.

How to Make a Budget

Spending without thinking is incredibly easy (and sometimes fun), but being organized and responsible with your money will spare you overdraft fees and maybe even allow you to save up for big purchases (or, um, retirement).

1. **Calculate your income.** Got a steady paycheck? This part's easy. Working part-time, flexible hours, or freelance? Calculate a busy month, then do the same for a dry spell, and split the difference to find your average monthly income.

2. **Calculate your fixed expenses.** *Fixed* means stuff you pay for every month, without exception: rent, food, utilities, insurance, and transportation costs. Include things like student loans, car payments, and 401(k) contributions if applicable.

3. **Subtract expenses from income.** Ideally, you should have some money left over (if not, go back and check your math!). This is your *expendable income*, which you can divvy up for other (read: fun) expenses.

4. **Keep track of how you spend.** Set up a monthly spreadsheet in a program like Microsoft Excel to track how you're spending that expendable income. Group or even color-code your expenses in broad categories: food, entertainment, home (rent, utilities, repairs), pets, fitness, work, and travel.

5. **Tweak as necessary.** Running into the red? Assign limits to your disposable-income categories and stick to them. Small changes, like making coffee at home instead of spending $6 on Starbucks, visiting your library instead of buying books, or packing a lunch, make a big difference.

6. **Save early, save often.** The goal of a budget is not to end up with a balanced zero dollars in your bank account at month's end. Once your spending habits are under control, start a savings account and earmark a little cash every month for emergencies—a parking ticket, surgery for your pet, a replacement computer—or long-term goals like a down payment on a car or house. Even if you won't be saving hundreds of dollars every month, having a nest egg will provide peace of mind.

7. **Handle windfalls wisely.** Earn a big bonus at work, receive an unexpected inheritance, or win the lottery? (It could happen!) Put the money toward outstanding debt *before* spending it on fun stuff.

How to Buy a Car

A car is one of the biggest purchases—physically and financially—you'll ever make. Knowing what you want and being informed will save you from getting ripped off or ending up with a subpar vehicle. Here's how to shop like a pro.

- Make a list (yes, on paper!) of what you want in terms of size, fuel efficiency, cost, ecofriendliness, transmission type, and mileage (if the car is used).

- A car is not a one-and-done purchase. When budgeting, consider monthly insurance premiums, title transfer and inspection fees, and fuel and repair costs.

- Consider buying used. New cars lose value just rolling out of the lot, and used cars—even those in pretty good shape—come much cheaper. Get the car's full vehicular pedigree—including the number of owners, accident history, any previous mechanical problems, and what repairs and maintenance have been done—from a third-party service like CarFax.

- Financing lets you pay a little at a time, as opposed to paying the full amount in cash, but usually involves spending more than the sticker price because of interest rates. Do the math first!

- Don't buy the first car you see, or even the fifth. Visit dealerships, browse online, and get an idea of prices and quality. Start shopping with no intention of buying; you can (and should) walk away for a day or two before signing on the dotted line. If anyone makes you feel pressured or guilty, or if the negotiation isn't going well, go elsewhere.

- And speaking of negotiating: once you've made a decision, don't accept the initial price. Use a resource like J. D. Power or the Kelley Blue Book to figure out the approximate price the dealer paid for the car—your first offer shouldn't be too much higher than that. Negotiate the "out-the-door price": the price with everything, even taxes, included. Nervous to haggle in person? Negotiate over email, and tell dealers that you'll come in person to sign paperwork only once the price is set.

- Car salespeople aren't as slimy as the stereotype, but you should keep your wits about you. Don't take anything a dealer says at face value, and don't let them play on your emotions (you can even ask them to be quiet during a test drive if they're pointing out too many perks).

- Read absolutely everything you sign. Don't agree to extra fees that may be tacked on at the end, and don't sign an "as is" statement (a document that states you agree to buy the car in whatever shape it's in at the moment). Make sure you get thirty days to test the car and return it if there are hidden flaws.

How to Tip

A friendly "thank you" is good, but a tip is better. The only time you shouldn't tip is if the person providing the service is the owner of the establishment. When abroad, make sure to read up on the local customs. Tipping varies by country.

- **Restaurants:** Unless the service was so horrible that you simply can't stomach the idea of giving money to your server (although many people will typically leave 10 percent in this situation), the general rule of thumb is 15 to 20 percent of the bill. Many establishments automatically add a gratuity to the bill for groups of six or more, in which case you don't need to add a tip.

- **Taxis and rideshare services:** Add a few dollars to the total. (Rideshare apps will often suggest three options.) If the driver got you there fast, helped you load eight suitcases, or otherwise went above and beyond, add another buck or two.

- **Valet parking:** The venue may suggest about five dollars, but remember that wages for these workers are low and they rely on tips. So if you're feeling flush, share the wealth.

- **Bars:** A dollar per drink is standard, although giving more might get you faster service for the next round.

- **Hotels:** Room service expects 10 to 15 percent. Give bellhops a few dollars per bag. It's up to you if you want to leave a tip for housekeeping, and the amount depends on the hotel and the length of your stay; leave cash on the dresser when you check out.

- **Manicures, haircuts, and other beauty treatments:** The usual amount is 10 to 20 percent. A good tip can also help get you squeezed in for a last-minute appointment when you need one.

- **Service staff:** It's customary to tip house cleaners, doormen, superintendents, and so forth around the holidays. The amount is entirely up to you, but a generous tip will help shoot you to the top of the list when you need help installing an air conditioner or new blinds.

INTERPERSONAL
STUFF

How to Make New Friends

You never had to think about making friends when you were a kid. It sort of just happened, and you can't remember exactly how you did it. But now, suddenly asking another person to get lunch with you sounds, well, creepy. But learning to make new friends is a crucial social skill—friendships are just as important as relationships (if not more). So how do you go about nurturing friendships without coming across as a stalker?

- **At work:** This is likely where you spend the majority of your time, so what better place to look for friends? You already share something in common, and if you connect on another level with a coworker, start small. Invite them to grab a midmorning coffee. Suggest a casual lunch if you're both stuck working through mealtime. Let friendships at the workplace develop naturally rather than coming on too strong.

- **Sports:** Gyms are highly social locations, especially if you take a group exercise class. Seeing the same people week after week provides the perfect opportunity for chitchat. Even better is joining an intramural adult league of a sport that you enjoy. You'll be getting exercise, plus team sports encourage social behavior. Most cities and towns have local running, hiking, or cycling clubs, or you can start one of your own on the internet. These will put you in contact with people who share a common interest, which is the first step in developing a connection.

- **Volunteer opportunities:** Helping others will allow you to foster connections with the people you're helping and with other volunteers. Many local organizations will match you up with an opportunity most suited to your time and interest level, helping groups dedicated to protecting or supporting children, the elderly, animals, low-income families, domestic-abuse survivors, the sick, or the environment.

- **Hobbies:** Whether your passion is crochet, art, music, wine tasting, gardening, comic-book collecting, poker, young professional societies—whatever—there's a club for it. Join! Attend a "sit and knit" at your local yarn shop. Sing in the choir at your church. Get involved with local government. Just as with dating, you're never going to meet anyone if you stay cooped up in your apartment with your cat. In this day and age, there is a club for nearly everything. Just look online to find what's available near you.

- **Classes:** If you don't have a hobby yet, maybe it's time to get a hobby? Learning a new sport, craft, language, or other pastime is a great way to meet people—and if you don't find a friend, you still come away with a new skill! Pick something you've always wanted to learn, and chances are that you'll have something in common with other people who share your interest.

- **Online:** Online isn't just for screaming into the void. You can also easily find people who share your interests—and some of them may even be local! Join a group for your neighborhood, or find a discussion board for your hobby. Or try out one of the dating-style apps that's meant for purely platonic connections. Just be sure to always be safe when meeting up with strangers by informing a friend or family member of your plans.

- **Friends of friends:** If a family member or friend (locally or in another city) knows someone who lives near you, ask for an introduction (even if it's just over email). You already have your mutual acquaintance in common, so you're more likely to hit it off. Also, there's a good chance they have qualities that you look for in a friend since they're already friends with someone you care about.

- **Everyday locations:** Don't discount libraries, coffee shops, the grocery store, or the train. People tend to have routines, so it's likely you'll see the same faces frequently. This gives you the perfect opportunity to strike up a conversation. Chat up your neighbors. Talk to the person you see every morning on your commute. Most people are generally friendly if you give them a chance.

Making friends might not be as easy or as natural as it was in school, but you just have to approach it in a different way. Make a point to put yourself in social environments where people are interacting. Sure, it might seem daunting at first to show up somewhere alone, but the more you put yourself out there, the more you'll feel comfortable in solo social situations. It's only a matter of time before you meet people with whom you connect.

- **Be proactive . . .** You'll have to make more of an effort to cultivate friendships than ever before, and that's all right. You don't need to be seducing these proto-pals, but do reach out to people, suggest activities, make definite plans, and follow up. Say "yes" and go out when invited. It all starts somewhere.

- **. . . but don't be too hard on yourself.** You won't hit it off with everyone you meet—right away, or ever. But if making new friends takes time, it's never been easier to keep in touch with your old ones.

How to Give and Accept a Compliment

"I love your shirt!"

"Oh, it's so wrinkled . . . I found it in the bottom of my closet, I never wear it because I don't like how it fits but I have no clean clothes and . . ."

Stop. None of this demoralizing drivel. Here's how to acknowledge a compliment and pay it forward.

- When someone compliments you, smile and say "thank you." You can throw in a witty (not self-derogatory!) response, if you're so inclined. But please, don't use the opportunity to deflect the praise or put yourself down.

- If the coworker who sits a few cubicles down from you is wearing a color that suits them, tell them so. Hearing your comment will make their day, and you'll feel good about making someone else feel good. It's win-win. But . . .

- Only give a compliment if you mean it. An insincere compliment is far worse than no compliment at all. You'll appear fake, and the other person will wonder why you're being a jerk. Even worse is overly complimenting someone in an attempt to suck up or make nice. People see right through it.

- Few people don't like hearing and talking about themselves. If you're introduced to a new person and the tone is chilly, flash a bright smile and find something to compliment. Odds are the interaction will warm up a little and the ensuing conversation will be that much more pleasant.

It pays to be nice. Always. If this skill doesn't come naturally, follow these simple guidelines.

1. **Be observant and specific.** Your attention to detail will make the compliment more meaningful. Example: "I admire your respect for the environment."

2. **Justify the compliment.** Your reason for giving the compliment will reinforce its sincerity. Example: "I admire your respect for the environment and the way you're taking steps to improve it."

3. **Use an example.** Cement your sincerity by recounting a story. Example: "I admire your respect for the environment and the way you're

taking steps to improve it. It was really great how you set up the recycling program at our office."

4. **Ask a question.** This can also act as a conversation starter. Example: "I admire your respect for the environment and the way you're taking steps to improve it. It was really great how you set up the recycling program at our office. Is there anything I can do to help?"

5. **Follow up later.** A thoughtful email or thank-you note is always appreciated. There's no need to be wordy. It's the thought that counts. Example: "Thank you so much for taking the time to show us how to sort our office recyclables. Your dedication to this project has been inspirational."

How to Make Small Talk

The art of small talk is one worth cultivating. Here are a few tips for navigating a cocktail hour or a slightly awkward office holiday party.

1. Smile. It will let people know you are receptive and friendly. You'll feel more comfortable striking up conversations with strangers if you stand up straight and act confident.

2. Start with something neutral that requires more than a one-word answer. If you're nervous, keep it simple: "So, how do you know Justin?" or "What's a good place to eat around here?" If you can't come up with an opener, pay the person a (sincere) compliment.

3. Ask lots of questions. Everyone likes talking about themselves.

4. If you've tried every trick in the book and Susie's still icy, maybe she's just having a bad day. Say you need to go grab another drink and move on to a friendlier stranger.

5. Sometimes friendliness can backfire, like when the office bore warms up to you at the holiday

party and starts giving you a detailed description of their collection of photos of telephone poles. In that case, tell them you have to go get some water or make sure your cube mate is going easy on the wine, and bow out gracefully. If you feel bad, rope someone else into the conversation and, after a minute, use your line and leave them to it.

Conversation Topics to Avoid with Strangers

1. Health issues

2. Long recaps of books or movies

3. Offensive or off-color jokes

4. Anything personal or embarrassing about you, your friend, or your significant other

5. Politics or religion

6. Money

How to Host a Dinner Party

Congratulations, you're about to entertain! Nothing says "I'm a functional adult" quite like inviting friends over for a mature evening of food and conversation. These tips will make the whole endeavor a rousing success.

- **Figure out the scope.** Decide how many guests are attending and how much work you're willing to put into the affair. Will this be a sit-down dinner or a the-more-the-merrier-style potluck? Manage everyone's expectations.

- **Send invitations.** Handwritten notes not necessary! Share the deets on social media or by email: what kind of meal you're serving, what guests should bring (if anything), and whether plus-ones are welcome.

- **For potlucks, plan ahead.** Coordinate with guests so that you don't end up with fourteen baguettes and no vegetables. Stock up on serving spoons—not everyone will remember to bring one—and ask everyone to label dishes for easy returning.

- **Keep the menu simple.** Avoid new-to-you recipes or anything that must be cooked in batches (no made-to-order omelets!) unless you want to be stuck in the kitchen all night. Be mindful of allergies and religious or dietary restrictions: a good host ensures everyone eats comfortably.

- **Shop early and smart.** Stock up ahead of time—you don't want to be running to stores the morning of the dinner party—and make sure you have staples like flour, oil, and sugar.

- **Get equipped.** Do you have all the requisite kitchen supplies? Enough dishes, glassware, cutlery, and seating? Borrow or buy whatever you need, and don't forget small essentials like ice and napkins (and, *ahem*, toilet paper).

- **Make a schedule.** Give yourself more time than you think you need to get all the food ready. Pay attention to the cooking times of recipes and do prep work as soon as you can (chop ingredients ahead of time, put in a bowl, and store in the fridge until needed). Bake desserts ahead (the morning of, or earlier) and pick no-cook appetizers for guests to munch on while waiting for the meal.

- **Set the mood.** Create ambiance with a playlist that's a few hours long and lively but not fist-pumpingly upbeat. Light a few candles, use a nice tablecloth, and if you have flowers or decorations you can use as a centerpiece, pull 'em out.

- **Host.** Your job isn't over once the food is out. Introduce guests to one another and help start conversations. If a wallflower is having a hard time mingling, pay attention to them for a while.

- **Take your time.** Don't immediately clean up after the food's gone. Linger at the table, make sure the conversation is flowing (by encouraging some and reining in others), and start washing dishes only once everyone has left.

How to Ask Someone Out

Asking a cute human being to go on a date is one of the hardest things: you're putting yourself out there and risking rejection. But the rewards are worth it. Here's how to pull it off successfully, you Casanova, you.

- **Make your interest clear.** Don't say you want to *hang out*. The object of your affection might think you mean spending time as friends. Make your request clear by asking, "May I take you out for dinner or drinks?" or by using the word *date*.

- **Keep things casual to start.** Work in your invitation near the end of a conversation, or send a quick text or online message. Sure, an in-person request is more special, but if you're having trouble getting the words out, sending a quick "Hey, would you be interested . . ." message is absolutely valid.

- **If yes, make firm plans.** No one wants to get asked to do "something" "sometime"—suggest a specific time and place. Dinner and a movie may be standard, but grabbing drinks or coffee is a better first-date option: it's casual and low commitment, and if things get awkward, you don't have to stick around for dessert or the closing credits. Sign off with a simple, optimistic "Can't wait!"

- **If no, handle rejection gracefully.** Getting turned down sucks, but remember that your crush doesn't owe you anything. *You* might think you're a match made in heaven, but the object of your affection is not required to date you or even to tell you *why* they're not interested. Say something along the lines of "Okay, no worries, have a good night," and don't push. Eventually you'll find someone who jumps at the chance to get to know you better.

How to Break Up

The end of a relationship is never fun, whether you're on the delivering end or the receiving end. When you're the one ending the relationship, be mindful of the other person's feelings and try to make the experience as painless as possible.

1. You can't end a relationship before you're ready, but once you make that decision, commit to it. If the other person isn't ready for the relationship to end, they will likely try to talk you out of it, so you need to be strong and confident in your decision.

2. Often making a list of all the negatives can help solidify your decision. Write down negative feelings, arguments, or specific examples of times when you felt crappy in the relationship. This will help you drive home your point that you two are not the best match.

3. Deliver the news in person. No emails, phone calls, or text messages. As tempting as it may be to be passive-aggressive, this is the cowardly way to deal with things. Be an adult. You owe this person an honest explanation.

4. Calmly explain your points in a clear, honest, and straightforward manner. Be firm but polite. Don't ridicule or berate the other person. Plainly state your reasons why you are ending the relationship.

5. Do not lead the person on or give them false hope. If you think they are a good person, pay them a compliment and tell them why they're a great catch. Avoid placing blame. Instead refer to the fact that you two just aren't a good fit. You want to indicate that the breakup is due to a mismatch, not a personal flaw.

6. Breakups can be dramatic and emotional. Try to keep your wits about you. The calmer you are, the calmer the other person will be as well. Some people can become irrational, overly dramatic, or even violent. If you sense that will be the case, meet in a public setting, such as a coffee shop, or have a nearby friend or relative on call to be there at a moment's notice.

7. Avoid feeling guilty or punishing yourself for your decision. Remind yourself of your reasons for choosing to end the relationship, referring back to your list of negatives if necessary.

8. "Let's still be friends" never works. You need some time and space apart before a friendship is possible. Someday you may be able to have that kind of bond with this person, but immediately after the breakup you need to make a distinction and create emotional distance. Avoid physical intimacy with this person after the breakup—that will only complicate the matter and lead to more pain.

How to Attend a Wedding

It's a fact of life: as people get older, people get married. And that's a good thing! Weddings are parties, a fun celebration of a wonderful milestone in the life of people you care about. And as with any institution that's been around a while, rules must be followed. Here's how conduct yourself so that everyone has a good time.

- **Confirm your attendance.** This is about more than being polite. A large wedding is a carefully orchestrated affair, and knowing the exact number of attendees is necessary. If the invitation notes an "RSVP by" date, respect it and let the couple know if you'll attend and whether you'll bring a date—if you've been offered that option (your invitation will be addressed to "Mr./Ms. [your name] and Guest" if so). Don't assume that a plus-one (or child) is welcome. If you have to cancel at the last minute, definitely alert the couple.

- **Give a gift.** If you attend the wedding, you should give a gift, period. The easiest way is to shop the couple's gift registry (usually listed on the website) for something within your budget, though a check with a nice card is fine. If you won't be attending, technically you're off the hook, but sending a card wishing them well is a nice gesture. Procrastinator? Conventional wedding etiquette allows you to give a gift up to a year after the wedding.

- **Be a team player.** If you're asked to be a part of the wedding as a bridesmaid, groomsman, or anything in between, congratulations! Before you commit, ask what the happy couple requires of you. You might be expected to attend dress shopping trips and prewedding festivities like bridal showers, bachelor parties, etc. Better to bow out early than be blindsided by a bride who expects you to buy a custom-made dress or a couple who presume you have an entire week to devote to their nuptials.

- **Dress the part.** The invitation should specify a dress code, but if not, a suit or cocktail dress will do the trick. Avoid wearing white (that's for the bride!), and use judgment with black—traditionally, it's reserved for funerals. If the ceremony will be at a religious site, dress appropriately— collars and ties, no bare shoulders or short hems. And wear shoes you can dance in!

- **Set boundaries** . . . Don't feel pressure to spend money you don't have on a destination wedding and endless bridal party events. If you're uncomfortable with portions of the proceedings (anything from a seedy bachelor party to a religious prayer), feel free to excuse yourself.

- **. . . but remember that it's not about you.** The bride might be bossy, the theme might be ridiculous, and the bar might be cash, but guess what: it's *their* special day. Be gracious. Don't snicker during speeches, stick around until the cake is cut, and thank the couple for inviting you, either during the receiving line (if there is one) or before the end of the night.

How to Have an Argument

Inevitably, you will disagree with your partner on something. Hopefully it's not too often. When it happens, it's critical that you approach the discussion in a healthy and productive manner in order to communicate properly and find common ground. Here's how to do it.

- **Consider the timing of the conversation.** Let's face it: there's no good time to argue. And certainly, these interactions can happen unexpectedly. But whenever possible, aim to have the conversation when both of you have enough time to talk and are able to focus. For example, don't bring up a conflict as your partner is leaving for an appointment. If the argument happens unexpectedly, suggest tabling the discussion until a better time. But don't avoid having the conversation completely.

- **Make the goal about reaching a compromise.** Trying to win the argument means your partner loses—which means you both lose. Instead, think about it as you and your partner against the problem—not each other. Figure out where you can budge and what elements are nonnegotiable.

That will likely leave a lot of gray area where you can find common ground with your partner.

- **Listen and ask questions.** Hearing your partner's point of view and asking clarifying questions will help move the conversation toward the goal of compromise. Use nonthreatening language like "Help me understand" to gather more information about how your partner is feeling and why.

- **Share your feelings.** Opening up about your thoughts will enable your partner to further understand your position and what's important to you. Avoid complaints like "you always . . . ," which can sound like accusations and put your partner on the defensive. Instead, make requests that rephrase the topic around you: "I'm stressed about not having time to make dinner each night. Would you mind helping me out on some of the nights?"

- **Remain respectful, calm, and on topic.** Avoid yelling, name-calling, and insulting each other. Resist the temptation to let unrelated issues or past arguments creep into the conversation. If you sense that things are getting too tense, suggest taking a break and revisiting the topic at a later time. Cool off, but don't avoid each other completely in the interim.

- **Know how to apologize.** This is someone you care about deeply. And the goal is to maintain a happy, balanced relationship. Different people and arguments may require different types of apologies. Some people want larger gestures, while others just want to know you've heard them and will do better.

How to Say No

No one likes to hear, or say, "no," but sometimes we have to do it—whether you're shutting down a whine from a kid, an invitation from a frenemy, or a request for help from a coworker when you're already overwhelmed.

- **Be firm.** When you say "no," mean it and do not relent, even if the other person wheedles or tries to reason you out of it. Be consistent in your tone and body language. You don't need to justify yourself—if the other person is argumentative, a repeated phrase like "that won't be possible" is plenty and won't offer them anything to pick apart.

- **Offer an alternative.** If this is a relationship you want to keep, make sure you aren't *only* saying "no." Friends, family, and children need to know that you do want to do things for and with them, just not that particular thing. Try including alternatives that you are willing or able to do: "I won't be able to watch your cat all weekend, but I'd love to get lunch when you're back."

- **Don't second-guess yourself . . .** It's natural to feel a little guilty about saying "no," especially if you have people-pleasing tendencies or the other person is argumentative (or a small child!). But remember that your worth does not depend on how much you are willing to do for people, or on how skillfully you can avoid ever disappointing them. If this relationship doesn't survive you saying "no" occasionally, maybe it didn't need to.

- **. . . but do notice if you're shutting down things that are good for you.** You can always turn down demands, invitations, and requests for favors that you can't (or just don't want to) take on. But if you're always in rejection mode, check in with yourself—are you being a good friend (or coworker, partner, or family member) generally? Is your life fulfilling overall? Sometimes we start defaulting to "no" as a way of avoiding connection or responsibility.

Enhance Your Adulthood
with the Stuff Series

Stuff Every Cook
Should Know

Stuff Every Gardener
Should Know

Stuff Every Wine
Snob Should Know

Stuff Every Cheese
Lover Should Know

Stuff Every Coffee
Lover Should Know